Japanese
Family-Style
Recipes

Japanese Family-Style Recipes

Hiroko Urakami

Photography by Hiroya Yoshimori

KODANSHA INTERNATIONAL
Tokyo • New York • London

Weights and Measures

To convert American linear and volume measurements used in the recipes in this book, refer to figures below. (Weights and temperatures are provided in both the metric and American system.)

1 American cup=240 ml
1 Japanese/British cup=200 ml
1 inch=2.5 centimeters

Food Styling by Kayoko Katoh

Distributed in the United States by Kodansha America, Inc., 575 Lexington Avenue, New York, N.Y. 10022, and in the United Kingdom and continental Europe by Kodansha Europe Ltd., 95 Aldwych, London WC2B 4JF. Published by Kodansha International Ltd., 17-14 Otowa 1-chome, Bunkyo-ku, Tokyo 112-8652, and Kodansha America, Inc.

99 00 01 02   15 14 13 12 11 10

ISBN 4-7700-1583-6

Library of Congress Cataloging-in-Publication Data

Urakami, Hiroko.
Japanese family-style recipes / Hiroko Urakami : photography by Hiroya Yoshimori.—1st ed.
        p.   cm.
Includes index.
ISBN 4-7700-1583-6
1. Cookery, Japanese.   I. Title.
TX724.5.J3U73 1991
641. 5952--dc20   91-41781

Contents

About Japanese Homecooking

This book introduces a style of Japanese cooking called *ofukuro no aji*, meaning "mother's cooking." It is like homecooking throughout the world, remembered nostalgically in adulthood and eaten with pleasure. Seasonings and ingredients may vary slightly from home to home, but the dishes remain basically the same.

In compiling the recipes for this book, I asked many of my foreign friends about the availability of Japanese ingredients, their ease of preparing particular types of foods, and their favorite dishes in Japan. While Japanese food is becoming increasingly popular overseas, Japanese restaurants and take-out shops abroad still serve a limited menu, leaving much of our home-style cooking untried and awaiting discovery. I hope these recipes will at last enable my many Western friends to cook the ordinary dishes they have come to love but were unable to enjoy when dining out. For the beginner chef, here is a brief overview of the different types of dishes found in Japanese homecooking.

Soups

Japanese soups are made from stock based on konbu seaweed and dried bonito flakes, and are a natural accompaniment to hot steamed rice. Miso soup, which contains miso and vegetables, is even popular at breakfast in Japan. Directions for making dashi stock can be found under "Cooking Notes," but there is no reason why you can't make your own stock from meat or other kinds of fish.

Seaweed and Vegetable Dishes, Including Salads

Vegetables in Japanese cuisine can be served raw, boiled, sautéed, sprinkled with vinegar, or dressed with various sauces or toppings. When braised in a soy sauce and sugar seasoning, vegetable dishes are less of a salad and more of a dish to accompany rice, usually with thought given to the nutritional balance of the meal. Seaweeds, such as hijiki and wakame, are a non-caloric, mineral-rich healthfood, and are excellent accompaniments to meat and fish dishes.

Tofu and Egg Dishes

Tofu is justly called the "meat of the fields," as it is made from highly nutritious soybeans. Because of its bland taste, tofu can be combined with many ingredients and seasonings to produce a variety of interesting main dishes. Eggs, too, play an important role in Japanese cooking, and dishes made from them have the advantage of using little or no vegetable oil, such as in Rolled Omelette or in Savory Egg Custard.

Fish, Meat, and Poultry Dishes

Dishes containing meat or fish are frequently the focal points of meals served in Japanese homes, although their portions will be much smaller than what you might be accustomed to. They are usually accompanied by a number of side dishes to make a nutritionally balanced meal. Being an island nation, fish is an important part of the Japanese diet. It is eaten raw or, in the case with large fish, also filleted and fried. Small, dark-meat fish rich in vitamin E, such as sardines, are braised, grilled, or deep-fried whole, or they may be filleted and pounded into a paste to make dumplings.

Meat, fish, or poultry simmered with lots of vegetables

in a large pot on the table is a classic dish eaten in winter with family and friends. Called *nabe ryori*, this one-pot cookery has regional variations, prescribing a different broth, ingredients, and seasonings.

Rice, Noodles, and Pancakes

If rice is to be the main focus of a meal, it can be prepared in a variety of different ways. *Donburi*, or meal-in-a-bowl, can contain a simmered meat, egg, and vegetable combination, or *sashimi* (raw fish), served on a bed of hot steamed rice. Beef Donburi is one of the most popular such dishes in Japan.

Another typical rice dish is seasoned rice, where white rice and other ingredients are cooked together. In autumn, seasoned rice with mushrooms, and in spring, one with bamboo shoots are prepared, expressing a time-honored appreciation of the seasons. In homes, seasoned rice is served with accompanying dishes, just like plain, steamed rice.

A third type of rice dish, sushi, uses vinegar-seasoned rice as a base for accompanying ingredients. The most well-known dish in this category might be *nigiri-zushi*, where slices of fresh raw fish and shellfish are placed over compact, bite-size mounds of cooled, white rice, or *maki-zushi*, where the ingredients, along with rice, are wrapped with crisp, nori seaweed.

Still another rice dish is Rice Balls, in which freshly steamed rice is sprinkled lightly with salt and a little vinegar, mixed well and shaped with the hands to a suitable size. It can then be wrapped with nori seaweed or sprinkled with sesame seeds for an appetizing, finger-food rice course.

Noodles are also frequently served in a wide variety of appetizing ways, using either *udon*, made from wheat flour; *soba*, made from buckwheat flour; or *ramen*, a Chinese-style wheat-and-egg noodle. These are either served in a hot broth, with a dipping sauce, or stir-fried with vegetables, and can provide a meal balanced in carbohydrates and protein and low in fats.

Finally, there are the savory Japanese-style pancakes, made from wheat flour, shredded cabbage, and any combination of vegetables, seafood, meat, or chicken.

Snacks and Desserts

Mochi, a pounded glutinous rice specialty, can be eaten either savory or sweet. It frequently replaces rice at meal times, or makes a delicious snack any time of the day. Mochi is prepared in a variety of ways. In this book, two much-loved recipes for dessert mochi are included, one covered with sweetened soybean powder, the other in azuki bean paste. If you appeal to your ingenuity, it might also become an interesting ingredient in casseroles, or serve as a tasty pizza base.

Also included are two favorite between-meal snacks, Sweet Potato Twists, made from puréed sweet potatoes, and Deep-Fried Sugar Cookies, which are crispy, puffy, and light. These, along with the sweet mochi desserts, are especially delightful when accompanied by cups of steaming hot green tea—an experience I hope you will have.

While I hope that you can follow the recipes with the listed ingredients, so that you'll get an idea of the taste of a dish, please don't give up if the exact ingredients are unavailable where you live. Make do with local produce, or with the seasoning substitutions recommended, and I think you'll end up with a dish surprisingly similar in taste to the original Japanese. Finally, and equally important, please remember to add that all-important ingredient love, which translates to joy and enthusiasm in your cooking adventure. This book, after all, is about cooking and eating good, wholesome foods with loved ones.

Cooking Notes

Steamed White Rice

Although many people have an automatic rice cooker for perfect steamed rice, if you don't own one of these conveniences, select a moderately large, thick pot with a well-fitting lid. Most of the rice recipes in this book will call for 7 cups steamed rice. To prepare this amount, you will need to cook 2-1/2 cups short-grain white rice. Wash the rice first by stirring it in water with your hand or a large wooden spoon. Drain the opaque water and repeat three or four times until the water becomes almost clear. Let the rice sit in 2-3/4 cups water for 30 minutes. This will plump up the grains and ready them for cooking. Cook the rice over medium heat, covered, until the water begins to boil. Then turn heat to low and simmer for another 10 minutes, or until there are "dimples" in the rice when you peek under the lid.

Remove from heat and let it stand, covered, to allow the rice to finish steaming for 5 minutes. Remove lid and toss the rice with a Japanese bamboo paddle or wooden spoon. Tossing allows the steam and air to circulate and makes the rice uniformly fluffy. Cover the pot with a dry dish towel and replace lid until ready to serve.

Note: When preparing basic steamed rice add 1-1/4 cups water for each cup short-grain white rice. If you prefer brown rice, which is chewy and richer in vitamins, increase the water to 1-3/5 cups for every 1 cup of rice and let simmer for 1 hour after boiling.

Japanese Broth

Dashi, or flavoring stock, an essential ingredient in Japanese dishes, is often made from dried bonito flakes and dried konbu kelp. Dashi concentrates are available as bouillon cubes, liquid concentrate, or granules and are handy when there isn't enough time to make stock from scratch. Since dashi is used not only in soups but in a wide variety of dishes ranging from sauces to braised entrées, it is convenient to have some always readily available. You may store dashi in the freezer, for example, and in the refrigerator, dashi will keep for 3 days.

To make dashi, soak a 4-inch strip of konbu kelp in 3-1/4 cups water for 1 hour, then place the kelp and soaking water in a saucepan over medium heat. Just before the water begins to boil take the kelp out. Add 1/2 cup dried bonito flakes and turn heat to low. Cook for 30 seconds, then remove from heat and strain, either with a fine strainer or with a sieve lined with cheesecloth. This is called *ichiban dashi*,

8

meaning "best stock," and is used as soup stock. Place the kelp and dried bonito flakes reserved from the *ichiban dashi* in a saucepan with 4 cups of water and bring to a boil. This strained liquid, called *niban dashi* (secondary stock), can be used for stews and simmered dishes. However, many busy cooks will often use the *ichiban dashi* as a flavoring stock for all dishes.

Favorite Japanese Seasonings: Soy Sauce, Sake, Mirin, Sugar, and Miso

Fresh, unadulterated ingredients need only a light touch of seasonings during cooking to bring out their natural flavors. If a dish is seasoned too strongly, adding more dashi broth or water will help to bring it back into balance.

Japanese cooking has long used soy sauce, made from soybeans, wheat, and salt, as a seasoning. Along with salt, soy sauce has also been used to preserve food. For example, peeled, whole garlic cloves might be preserved immersed in a bottle of soy sauce, or soy sauce might be used in pickled vegetables. When added to stews and simmered dishes in the beginning of the cooking process, the salt in the soy sauce keeps the outsides of ingredients firm longer, serving a useful purpose, for example, in simmering tender-meat fish, such as sardines, pike, and mackerel, where the meat is prevented from falling apart. Usually, however, soy sauce is added after ingredients have become tender.

Sugar or seasoning containing sugar, such as mirin, have the effect of tenderizing foods, besides adding flavor. For this reason, it is usually added in the beginning of the cooking process, allowing other seasonings added later to become more easily absorbed.

Sake (rice wine), through its amino acids, also serves to tenderize foods in cooking. It counteracts strong odors (thus being especially useful in cooking fish or meat), and also brings out the natural flavors of foods, helping other seasonings to mingle and marry well. However, it is not always necessary to use sake each time to produce delicious results.

Mirin, a very sweet wine made from glutinous rice, is used only in cooking. It imparts a mildly sweet flavor and pleasing sheen in cooking, as in teriyaki sauce and yakitori (skewered grilled chicken). When mirin is not available, combine one tablespoon sake with one teaspoon sugar for every tablespoon of mirin.

Miso, a fermented soybean paste made with rice, barley, or soybean malt, is used frequently in the beginning or at the end of the cooking process. It is a good seasoning to use in soups, dressings, and grilled and pan-fried foods. It is especially delicious used in simmering fish dishes. Since overcooking will result in a bitter taste, one technique is to add the miso during cooking in two stages. Miso is a good alternative to salt in cooking: on average, one tablespoon of miso is equivalent to 1/2 teaspoon of salt.

A Japanese Family-Style Meal

A typical Japanese meal consists of a variety of foods, including a main dish of fish or meat, a side dish of braised vegetables, a vinegared salad, accompanied by steamed rice and soup (either miso soup or clear soup). Although the number of side dishes may vary according to the occasion, there will usually be a nice balance of flavors, textures, and colors, and rice and soup will always complete the meal.

The presentation of food and its visual appeal is as important in Japanese cuisine as the pleasure it gives to the palate, and in homecooking, this philosophy is not forgotten. In contrast to the Western custom of serving dishes in strict order, such as soup coming before the main course, the Japanese usually lay all dishes on the table at once, making a mouth-watering statement to tantalize appetites. Then, too, rather than arranging the foods on several large serving platters, individual portions are served on small dishes, each one selected for its size and shape. Second servings are uncustomary, except for rice and soup.

In recent years, Japanese cooking has become Westernized to a degree, and one or two large serving dishes may substitute for many small individual ones. Nevertheless, an assortment of small tableware remains characteristic of the Japanese table.

The typical Japanese supper (left) for one includes the essential steamed rice and soup, in this case miso soup made of tofu and mitsuba leaves (trefoil). These are supplemented by a deep-fried meat dish, simmered vegetable dish, and vinegared salad. (See Wakame Seaweed Miso Soup, Pork Cutlet Donburi, Simmered Squash, and Wakame Seaweed and Cucumber Salad for basic recipes.)

NUTRITIONAL ANALYSIS PER SERVING

Name of Dish	Calories	Protein(g)	Sodium(mg)	Fat(g)	Name of Dish	Calories	Protein(g)	Sodium(mg)	Fat(g)
Vegetable Chowder	215	10	2	7	Sautéed Burdock	123	2	2	4
Sardine Dumpling Soup (3 oz. sardines)	219	20	2	6	Braised Daikon	107	2	2	——
Wakame Seaweed Miso Soup	66	4	2	3	Braised Five Vegetables	248	12	2	7
Leafy Greens with Sesame Dressing	57	5	1	4	Vegetable Tempura	275	8	2	20
Spinach Ohitashi	36	5	1	——	Sautéed Mixed Vegetables	172	7	2	10
Wakame Seaweed and Cucumber Salad	51	5	1	——	Braised Hijiki	88	2	2	4
Salad with Tofu Dressing	186	11	1	6	Sushi in a Pouch	844	23	4	5
Yellowtail Teriyaki	377	23	3	23	Sushi Mélange	537	11	3	3
Miso-Braised Mackerel (1/4 lb portion)	345	25	3	20	Roll-Your-Own Sushi*	100–150	(varies)	(varies)	(varies)
Sardines Simmered in Ginger Sauce	275	19	2	14	Rice Balls	395	6	3	1
Breaded Fried Swordfish	271	23	1	12	Rice with Bamboo Shoots	495	10	1	9
Marinated Spicy Fresh-Water Smelt	223	17	1	13	Salmon Tea Rice	222	12	2	3
Sukiyaki	695	35	3	47	Chicken Rice Soup	192	10	1	5
Shabu-Shabu	597	39	3	44	Beef Donburi	560	21	2	14
Braised Meat and Potatoes	225	7	2	9	Chicken-and-Egg Donburi	773	23	3	8
Stuffed Chinese Cabbage Rolls	163	10	1	7	Pork Cutlet Donburi	789	27	4	15
Beef Liver and Sesame Sauté	139	16	1	10	Three-Colored Donburi	444	24	2	10
Yakitori	291	22	2	13	Chilled Soba Noodles with Nori	345	10	4	——
Chicken Mizutaki (7 oz. boneless chicken)	343	38	2	19	Summer Udon Noodles	574	18	6	8
Crystal Tofu	105	6	2	4	Japanese Stir-Fried Noodles	489	20	3	9
Tofu and Vegetable Scramble	136	8	1	7	Savory Supper Pancakes	402	28	1	16
Deep-Fried Tofu	180	8	2	7	Mochi Cakes (2 cakes / 3-1/2 oz. portion)	385	9	14	4
Tofu Croquette	215	7	1	17	Dessert Rice Balls (with azuki bean paste)	501	14	——	2
Rolled Omelette	125	9	1	6	White Dumplings	172	2	1	——
Savory Egg Custard	97	10	1	4	Deep-Fried Sugar Cookies	245	5	——	6
Grilled Eggplant with Ginger & Bonito Flakes	28	2	2	——	Sweet Potato Twists	236	2	——	3
Simmered Squash	108	2	1	——					

*One average-size hand roll with a slice of sashimi and vegetable

Ingredients	Amount	Calories	Protein (g)	Sodium (mg)	Fat(g)
Steamed white rice	1 cup (140 g)	207	5	——	1
Glutinous rice (uncooked)	1/4 cup (50 g)	173	4	——	——
Soy sauce	1 tablespoon	10	1	3	——
Low-salt soy sauce	1 tablespoon	9	1	2	——
Azuki beans, boiled	3-1/2 oz. (100 g)	143	9	——	1
Miso	1 tablespoon	34	2	2	1

Note: All figures are approximate. Negligible quantities are indicated by a dash (——).

Vegetable Chowder *(KENCHIN-JIRU)*

This delicious chowder contains tofu, a variety of vegetables, and some chicken simmered in a miso broth. By adding rice to the leftover broth, you have a tasty gruel. Beef, pork, or beans may be substituted for the chicken, or try a seafood chowder using your favorite fish or crustaceans.

In a large skillet, sauté the chicken, carrot, onion, and potato in sesame oil over medium-low heat for 2 minutes. When all ingredients are well coated with oil, add the dashi broth. When the dashi comes to a boil, remove any scum on the surface, add sake, and lower heat. Dissolve 2 tablespoons of miso in a few tablespoons of broth and add to the skillet. When vegetables have softened, add soy sauce, tofu, and the remaining miso dissolved in broth. Serve garnished with green onions and a dash of red chili pepper.

Serves 4 as a soup course.

3 ounces (85 g) boned, skinless chicken, cut into bite-size pieces
1 small carrot, peeled and cut into half rounds
1 medium onion, cut into chunks
1 medium potato, peeled and cut into half rounds
1-1/2 tablespoons sesame oil (OR vegetable oil)
5 cups dashi broth, chicken consommé, OR water
1 tablespoon sake
4 heaping tablespoons miso
1 teaspoon soy sauce
1 cake (10 oz/300 g) firm tofu, cut into 1/2-inch cubes
2 green onions, chopped
Dried Japanese red chili pepper (togarashi)

Photo on following page

Sardine Dumpling Soup *(IWASHI DANGO NO SUUPU)*

Highly nutritious dark-meat fish give off a strong odor when grilled or braised, but when boiled in soup, as in this dish, the odor is reduced. I've used sardines here, but lean ground chicken, shaped into dumplings, works equally well. This versatile soup lends itself to alternative flavorings, such as curry powder or paprika. The addition of corn starch at the end will thicken the soup, helping to keep it hot longer.

Have your fishmonger gut and fillet the sardines. Place the fillets on a cutting board and dice into small pieces. Transfer to a mortar and grind with a pestle, or use a food processor to make a paste. Add the seasoning ingredients and mix well. Shape the mixture into small dumplings (see photo).

Heat the dashi broth and add the dumplings. When the broth begins to boil, add the remaining soup ingredients and cook for 3 to 4 minutes until the dumplings surface and change color. Skim the surface of any scum and garnish with a sprinkling of chopped green onion.

Serves 4 as a soup course.

8 medium sardines

Seasoning for sardines:
1 teaspoon ginger juice (squeeze from freshly grated ginger)
1/2 tablespoon miso
2 teaspoons sake
1-1/2 tablespoons all-purpose flour

5 cups dashi broth OR fish stock
1 tablespoon sake
1 teaspoon soy sauce
1/3 teaspoon salt
Green onion OR watercress, chopped fine for garnish

Photo on preceding page

Wakame Seaweed Miso Soup *(WAKAME NO MISO-SHIRU)*

Usually accompanied by steamed rice, miso soup usually contains two or three ingredients. The most popular are tofu, carrots, onions, daikon, potatoes, eggplants, sweet potatoes, pork, chicken, or leafy green vegetables. Any type of miso can be used, dark or light, salty or less salty, or even a combination of these. If you use a milder flavored miso, increase the amount for a full-bodied taste. 1/2 cup milk may also be added for a mellow taste. The important point to remember is that once miso has been added to the soup, avoid boiling for more than a few seconds.

Rinse deep-fried tofu pouch in hot water to remove excess oil and slice thin. In a saucepan, bring the dashi broth to a boil; reduce heat and add the miso dissolved in a few tablespoons of broth. Add the tofu pouch slices, wakame seaweed, and sake, and bring to a boil for a few seconds before removing from heat. Adjust taste as necessary.* Serve in individual bowls, each garnished with three or four mitsuba leaves.

*If your miso soup tastes too salty, add more dashi broth or water. If you find it too mild, add 1 to 1-1/2 teaspoons soy sauce.

Serves 4 as a soup course.

1 deep-fried tofu pouches (abura-age)
3-1/2 cups dashi broth
4 heaping tablespoons miso
1/2 ounce dried wakame seaweed, softened in water for several minutes, rinsed well, and cut into 2-inch lengths
2 teaspoons sake
Several sprigs mitsuba (trefoil; OR chopped green onion) for garnish

Photo on following page

Leafy Greens with Sesame Dressing

(AONA NO GOMA-AE)

This salad may be made from a wide range of leafy green vegetables, including komatsuna (a kind of Chinese cabbage), chrysanthemum leaves (*shungiku*), spinach, and watercress. The sesame seeds are roasted before grinding to bring out the flavor in an aromatic, delicious dressing. When roasting, be sure to tilt the pan back and forth to avoid burning the seeds. Unused roasted seeds can be kept in a jar or sealed plastic container, although it's best to use them within two months (sooner if they have been ground). Sesame seeds are rich in vitamin E, which helps to promote anti-aging mechanisms in the body. If you don't have sesame seeds handy, try roasted, ground almonds or cashew nuts.

Wash and rinse the greens. Bring a large pot of water to a boil, add a pinch of salt, then add the greens, with stem ends at bottom and leafy parts at top. Boil for about 1 minute, then rinse under cold water. Bunch the stem ends together and squeeze out the water with your hands. This should be done thoroughly, or water will seep out when combined with the sesame dressing. Trim off ends and cut the bunch into 1-1/2-inch lengths.

Combine ground sesame seeds with sugar and soy sauce. Just before serving, mix the greens with sesame dressing.

Serves 4 as a salad course.

1 bunch (12 oz/350 g) leafy greens
A pinch of salt
3 tablespoons sesame seeds, roasted and
    ground
1-1/2 tablespoons sugar
1 tablespoon soy sauce

Photo on preceding page

Spinach Ohitashi *(HORENSO NO OHITASHI)*

This versatile salad is suited to any vegetable that requires boiling before being dressed, such as watercress or Chinese cabbage. Be generous with the bonito flake topping, as it is a good source of protein and adds a wonderful flavor to vegetables.

Wash the spinach carefully, especially around the stem ends where dirt and grit accumulate. Bring water to a boil in a large pot and add a pinch of salt. Add the spinach, with stem ends at bottom and leafy parts at top, and parboil about 1-1/2 minutes, or until tender but firm. Immerse immediately in cold water to seal in color. Gather the stem ends together and squeeze out the liquid with your hands. Cut into 1-1/2-inch lengths, discarding stem ends. Arrange in a shallow bowl. Combine the soy sauce and dashi broth and drizzle over the spinach. Serve topped with bonito flakes.

Serves 4 as a salad course.

12 ounces (350 g) spinach
A pinch of salt
2 tablespoons soy sauce
2 tablespoons dashi broth
1 cup dried bonito flakes (katsuo-bushi)

Photo on following page

Wakame Seaweed and Cucumber Salad

(OSU NO MONO)

This piquant salad balances flavor and color when served with other vegetables or with meat or fish courses. Celery or tomatoes, and fruits, such as persimmons or apples, are also tasty salad ingredients. Wakame seaweed, rich in calcium and dietary fiber, is a non-caloric vegetable, well suited to a vinegary dressing. Be sure to mix the dressing just before serving, or the salad will turn watery.

Pour boiling water over the wakame seaweed, then immerse immediately in cold water to retain color. Drain and sprinkle 1 tablespoon vinegar over the seaweed.

Sprinkle salt over the cucumber slices, let stand for 5 minutes until soft and watery, then squeeze out excess water.

Blanch shirasuboshi in boiling water, drain, and sprinkle with 1 tablespoon vinegar.

Combine the vinegar, sugar, and soy sauce and stir until the sugar dissolves. Mix in the cucumber, shirasuboshi, and wakame seaweed. Garnish with shredded ginger and serve immediately.

Serves 4 as a salad course.

3 ounces (90 g) fresh wakame seaweed, sliced into 2-inch lengths
5 plus 2 tablespoons rice vinegar
1/3 teaspoon salt
2 small cucumbers, sliced thin
2 ounces (55 g) shirasuboshi (dried tiny sardines), OR canned salmon or tuna flakes, shreds of crab meat, or boiled chicken
2 tablespoons sugar
1/2 teaspoon soy sauce
1-inch fresh ginger, peeled and shredded for garnish

Photo on preceding page

Salad with Tofu Dressing *(TOFU NO SHIRA-AE)*

This salad requires draining the tofu of much of its water content. The quickest method is to place the block of tofu on a plate and microwave on high for 3 minutes. Another quick way is to boil the tofu in a saucepan filled with water for about 3 minutes, take the tofu out and, when you can handle it comfortably, wrap in a clean kitchen towel and squeeze. Yet another method is to place the tofu on a plate with a heavy plate or similar object on top and let it stand for about 1 to 1-1/2 hours. Once made into a paste, tofu will keep 2 days in the refrigerator, or about 20 days in the freezer. Tofu paste is also tasty spread over toast or crackers.

Simmer carrot, konnyaku, tofu pouch, snow peas, and mushroom in the flavoring stock for 6 to 7 minutes, or until carrot strips are tender. Drain.

In a mortar, grind the sesame seeds with a pestle, then add the drained cake of tofu and remaining paste ingredients and blend well. If the mixture is too runny, add more ground sesame seeds.

Combine the boiled vegetables with the tofu paste. Serve chilled or at room temperature.

Serves 4 as a salad course.

1 small carrot, cut into julienne strips
1/2 cake konnyaku (devil's tongue), boiled and
    cut into bite-size pieces
1 deep-fried tofu pouch (abura-age), rinsed in
    boiling water and sliced thin
6 snow peas, cut into julienne strips and boiled
    until tender
1 dried mushroom, soaked for 30 minutes and
    cut into julienne strips

Flavoring stock:
1-1/2 cups dashi broth
1 tablespoon soy sauce
1 tablespoon sugar
1 tablespoon sake

Tofu paste:
3 tablespoons white sesame seeds, roasted
1 cake (10 oz/300 g) firm tofu, well drained
    (see above)
3 tablespoons sugar
1/2 teaspoon salt
1/4 teaspoon soy sauce

Photo on following page

Yellowtail Teriyaki *(BURI NO TERIYAKI)*

Yellowtail teriyaki is a classic pan-fried or grilled fish entrée, as popular in top Japanese restaurants as it is in the home, especially in the colder months from September through March, when the mature yellowtail is succulent and fat. Soy sauce is used in the sauce to give a slightly scorched aroma and a glossy finish to the fish. This method of cooking, called teriyaki, can be used with excellent results for other types of fish, meat, and poultry. If you prefer, after marinating the fillets, place them on a wire rack and broil in the oven (or grill over the stove top) instead of cooking them in the frying pan. You won't need the vegetable oil in this case, and the use of the rack will allow the fat to drip off, making for fewer calories—and it will be just as delicious.

Mix the ingredients for the marinade. In a flat dish, marinate the yellowtail fillets for 30 minutes. Then, lightly dust the fillets with flour, reserving the marinade.

Place the fillets in a heated frying pan with vegetable oil and cook about 2 minutes each side over medium-high heat. Place the fillets on individual serving dishes. Combine teriyaki sauce ingredients with the leftover marinade and bring to a boil in a saucepan. Remove from heat. Pour some of the teriyaki sauce over each fillet and serve immediately.

Serves 4 as a main dish.

Marinade:
3 tablespoons soy sauce
3 tablespoons sake
1 tablespoon sugar
2 teaspoons ginger juice (squeeze from freshly grated ginger)

4 yellowtail fillets (about 1/4 lb/115 g each)

Flour for dusting over fillets
2 tablespoons vegetable oil

Teriyaki sauce:
1 tablespoon sugar
3 tablespoons sake
1 tablespoon soy sauce

Photo on preceding page

Miso-Braised Mackerel *(SABA NO MISO-NI)*

This versatile method of cooking fish is especially delicious with the dark-fleshed variety, such as other types of mackerel or sardines. If these are unavailable, try herring or salmon. Miso will enhance the flavor of the fish, but if you don't have miso, braising with soy sauce and ginger will also produce good results. The ginger removes the fishy odor, so use it generously.

Place fish fillets in a strainer and pour boiling water over them to firm the flesh and to eliminate some of the fishy odor. Place the fillets in water in which sake has been added, and cook over medium heat for 2 minutes, until boiling. You may either add the ginger at this point, or use it later as a garnish. When the fillets are half-cooked (after about 5 minutes), add mirin, sugar, and miso dissolved in a little cooking broth. Lower heat and cook for 7 to 8 minutes more, or until the fish is done and the broth is thickened. Serve on individual plates and garnish with ginger shreds (if you haven't added them during the cooking).

Serves 4 as a main dish.

4 mackerel fillets (about 1/4 lb/115 g each)
1 cup water
1/2 cup sake
2 tablespoons mirin
3 tablespoons sugar
4 tablespoons miso
1-inch fresh ginger, peeled and shredded

Photo on following page

Sardines Simmered in Ginger Sauce

(IWASHI NO SHOGA-NI)

The oil of dark-meat fish, such as sardines, is known to contain high levels of beneficial extra-polyunsaturated fats, known as Omega-3s, which help to reduce the likelihood of cardiac problems and strokes. They are also rich in protein, vitamins, and minerals, making them a valuable addition in any health-promoting diet. This recipe introduces a simple and delicious way to eat sardines. The leftovers keep well in the freezer, so you might want to make extra portions. I sometimes decrease the soy sauce in the simmering sauce and add extra vinegar or lemon juice at the end to reduce the salt content.

Gut the fish, remove heads and rinse well. Slice larger sardines in two. In a wide, shallow pot, combine the sardines, ginger, water, and other sauce ingredients, except the rice vinegar, and cook over medium heat, basting the sardines with the sauce now and then. When the sauce begins to boil add the vinegar. Cook for another minute, and serve at room temperature in a large shallow bowl topped with ginger sauce.

8 sardines
1-inch fresh ginger, peeled and slivered
1-1/4 cups water
3 tablespoons soy sauce
6 tablespoons sake
3 tablespoons sugar
1-1/2 tablespoons mirin
1 tablespoon rice vinegar

Serves 4 as a side dish.

Photo on preceding page

Breaded Fried Swordfish *(SAKANA NO FURAI)*

Even less than enthusiastic fish eaters will be tempted by these light, crispy, deep-fried fish fillets. Any fresh, fish fillets, such as salmon or horse mackerel, can be used. If you're watching calories, fry the fish in a frying pan with a small amount of oil to a toasty brown and finish the cooking in the oven.

Sprinkle the steaks with salt and pepper. Dust each piece lightly with flour, dip in beaten egg, and coat evenly with breadcrumbs.

Heat vegetable oil to about 340° F (170° C). Fry the steaks until light golden color and drain on paper towels. Arrange deep-fried fillets on a serving platter and garnish with cherry tomatoes and watercress. Serve hot with the Worcestershire sauce.

Serves 4 as a main dish.

4 swordfish steaks
Salt and pepper
A little flour for dusting over fish
1 egg, beaten
Breadcrumbs for coating fish
Vegetable oil for deep-frying
Cherry tomatoes for garnish
A few sprigs of watercress for garnish
Worcestershire sauce

Photo on following page

Marinated Spicy Fresh-Water Smelt

(WAKASAGI NO NANBAN-ZUKE)

In 16th-century Japan, people from southern European countries, such as Spain and Portugal, were called *nanban-jin* (meaning "southern barbarians") and their products, *nanban no shinamono*. These foreigners favored using ground black pepper or red chili peppers in their cooking and in time such dishes came to be called *nanban-zuke*. This dish is a legacy from those times, using just a hint of red chili peppers. Excellent as an accompaniment to wine or sake, this dish keeps 5 to 7 days in the refrigerator. It can also be frozen.

Clean and gut the smelts, then rinse and pat dry. Sprinkle with salt and pepper. Dust lightly with flour and deep-fry in 3 inches of vegetable oil at 340°F (170° C) until fish turns a golden brown.

Mix the marinade ingredients in a saucepan and heat to a boil. Remove from heat.

In a large dish, place the fried smelt and onions in the marinade and let sit for 30 minutes or more. Serve chilled or at room temperature.

Serves 4 as an appetizer or side dish.

20 fresh-water smelts (OR horse mackerel fillets
    cut into slices)
Salt and pepper
Flour for dusting smelts
Vegetable oil for deep-frying

Marinade:
5 tablespoons rice vinegar
2 tablespoons soy sauce
2 tablespoons water
1-1/2 tablespoons sugar
1 dried Japanese red chili pepper (togarashi),
    seeds removed and chopped fine

5 small onions, sliced into thin rounds

Photo on preceding page

Sukiyaki *(SUKIYAKI)*

In former days, farmers working in the fields would grill pieces of chicken or meat on a spade called *suki*. Grilling meat in a heavy cast-iron pot came to be known as *sukiyaki*. Eventually an assortment of vegetables was added and the ingredients cooked in a sweet soy sauce broth, making this dish both nutritious and filling. Although lightly beaten raw egg is traditionally used as a dipping sauce, sukiyaki can be enjoyed without it, too. Various types of vegetables may be used, and just about any thinly sliced meat (except mutton) or poultry will go well in the pot. A bowl of steamed rice rounds out this meal.

Combine broth ingredients in a saucepan, bring to a boil, and set aside.

Arrange the meat, green onions, shirataki, tofu, and chrysanthemum leaves decoratively on a large platter. Break an egg into each of 4 individual serving bowls and lightly whisk.

Heat a cast-iron pot set on a portable gas or electric burner (use a deep-dish electric hot plate, if you don't have either one) at the dinner table and coat it well with beef suet. Add 2 or 3 slices of meat, some green onions, shirataki , and tofu, and sauté for a minute or so before adding 1/3 of the cooking broth. Add a portion of the chrysanthemum leaves. Diners help themselves to whatever they want as the ingredients are cooked. (Dip the food into an individual serving bowl containing the whisked egg before eating.) Add more meat, tofu, vegetables, and broth to the pot as the meal progresses. Adjust the seasoning of the broth to taste by adding more sugar, soy sauce, dashi or hot water (but be careful not to add too much water or the flavors of the meat will be diluted). Serve with steamed rice.

Serves 4 as a complete meal when accompanied by rice.

Broth:
1-1/2 cups dashi broth
3–4 tablespoons sugar
5 tablespoons soy sauce
3 tablespoons mirin
2 tablespoons sake

1-1/2 pounds (750 g) flank steak, sliced paper-thin
20 green onions OR 5 Japanese naga-negi (long onion) if available, cut into 1-1/2-inch lengths
2 bundles shirataki (devil's tongue noodles), boiled for 3 minutes and cut into 3-inch lengths
1 cake (10 oz/300 g) firm tofu OR grilled tofu if available, cut into large cubes
1 bunch chrysanthemum leaves (shungiku; OR spinach or watercress), rinsed and cut in half
Beef suet (OR vegetable oil)
4 eggs (optional)

Photo on following page

Shabu-Shabu *(SHABU-SHABU)*

This is another versatile one-pot meal that may be made with any vegetables you have on hand. Paper-thin slices of beef are dropped into a simmering pot of dashi broth and cooked for a few seconds by swishing them back and forth. (In fact, *shabu-shabu* is the onomatopoeic word for the sound made as morsels of meat are gently swished in the steaming broth.) Much of the fat on the beef dissolves when cooked like this, and the meat is eaten dipped in a tangy sauce. Although beef is traditionally used, you can substitute with lean cuts of pork or chicken. One way to end the meal is to add precooked rice or udon noodles to the leftover broth to make a tasty gruel.

Make the dipping sauces. If you feel adventurous, you might like to try your favorite barbecue sauce. Divide dipping sauces into individual serving bowls.

Arrange the meat, tofu, and vegetables decoratively on a large platter and set beside your electric skillet or hot pot on the dining table. Bring the dashi broth (enough to fill the pot) to a boil. At this point, each diner picks up a slice of meat, rinses it briefly in the hot broth until the meat changes color, then dips it in one of the dipping sauces.

Someone can take charge of adding vegetables and tofu, a little at a time, letting them simmer in the broth until cooked. Replenish broth as necessary by adding either more dashi broth or hot water to the pot.

After the meat and vegetables have been eaten, you can either serve the remaining broth as a clear soup, or add precooked udon noodles or rice to round off the meal. Let the noodles or rice cook in the hot broth for 2 to 3 minutes before serving.

Serves 4 as a complete meal when accompanied by noodles or rice.

Dipping sauce #1:
4 tablespoons fresh lemon juice
3 tablespoons soy sauce
6 tablespoons broth from the pot

Dipping sauce #2:
4 tablespoons white sesame seeds, roasted and ground
6–8 tablespoons mayonnaise

1 pound 10 ounces (750 g) beef sirloin, sliced paper-thin
1 block (about 10 oz/300 g) firm tofu, sliced into thin pieces
8 green onions OR 2 Japanese naga-negi (long onion) if available, sliced into 2-inch pieces
4 large leaves Chinese cabbage, sliced into 2-inch pieces
1 bunch spinach (about 10 ounces), washed and cut into half
6 cups dashi broth (OR beef or chicken consommé, or water)
1 pound precooked udon noodles OR 4–5 cups steamed rice (optional)

Photo on preceding page

Braised Meat and Potatoes *(NIKU-JAGA)*

This slightly sweet, soy sauce–based dish is a wonderful accompaniment to plain steamed rice, and it makes use of spring's freshly harvested potatoes, onions, and green peas. All the vegetables are braised in one large pot, allowing the different flavors to intermingle, and although the potatoes might become so tender as to fall apart, this does not detract from the dish. Equally adaptable to beef or chicken, every Japanese home has a favorite *niku-jaga* recipe.

Stir-fry the onion, pork, carrot, potatoes, and ginger in vegetable oil in a heavy skillet over low heat for 3 to 4 minutes. Combine the sugar, soy sauce, sake, and dashi broth in a mixing bowl and add to the pork and vegetables. Continue to cook over low heat, until most of the liquid is absorbed. Add the green peas and cook a few minutes more, or until the peas are tender. Serve hot.

Serves 4 as a side dish.

1 medium onion, cut into wedges
5 ounces (140 g) boneless pork loin, sliced thin
1 small carrot, cut into wedges
2 medium potatoes, pared and quartered
1/2-inch fresh ginger, peeled and shredded
1 tablespoon vegetable oil
2 tablespoons sugar
2 tablespoons soy sauce
2 tablespoons sake
1 cup dashi broth
3 tablespoons green peas

Photo on following page

Stuffed Chinese Cabbage Rolls *(HAKUSAI-MAKI)*

This is a hearty dish to prepare in winter, when Chinese cabbage is plentiful on the market. These nutritious leaves are wrapped around a mixture of ground meat, mushrooms, bamboo shoots, carrot, and egg and cloaked in a sauce of sake, soy sauce, and sugar. Substitute with regular cabbage or some other leafy vegetable such as lettuce, if you wish, or increase and vary the stuffing ingredients for adventurous eating. Try serving a white sauce with the stuffed cabbage, or substitute fish paste for the meat for a different taste experience.

Mix the ground meat, bamboo shoot, and shiitake mushrooms and add the filling seasonings. Divide the mixture into 8 portions and shape into ovals.

Scrape away the hard core of the cabbage leaves to make them easier to roll, then lightly dust the insides with flour. Place 1 portion of meat filling into each cabbage leaf and roll, securing each roll with a toothpick. Place stuffed cabbage rolls, carrot strips, dashi broth, soy sauce, sugar, sake, and salt in a saucepan. Loosely cover the saucepan with aluminum foil to allow some of the liquid to evaporate and cook over medium heat for 15 minutes. Serve topped with the sauce and garnished with carrot strips.

Serves 4 as a main dish.

5 ounces (150 g) ground pork and ground beef
    (OR ground beef only)
1-1/2 ounces (45 g) bamboo shoot, diced
3 fresh shiitake mushrooms diced (OR dried
    mushrooms, soaked in water for 30
    minutes)

Seasoning for filling:
1 egg
1 tablespoon corn OR potato starch
1/3 teaspoon soy sauce
1/5 teaspoon salt

8 leaves Chinese cabbage, blanched and
    drained
A little flour
8 toothpicks
1 small carrot, cut into julienne strips
2 cups dashi broth, OR consommé
1/2 tablespoon soy sauce
1/2 tablespoon sugar
3 tablespoons sake
1/2 teaspoon salt

Photo on preceding page

Beef Liver and Sesame Sauté *(GYUREBA NO GOMA ITAME)*

Liver has an established position in Western food repertoire, but it is just as tasty cooked Japanese style. Whether using beef, pork, or chicken liver, always rinse off all the blood before cooking to diminish the strong odor. Some cooks take it one step further by soaking the liver in milk, although the use of certain seasonings, such as sesame seeds, ginger, or miso work just as well in eliminating odor. An alternative method of cooking liver in this recipe without using as much vegetable oil is to boil it for 5 minutes in a pot of water containing ginger peel, celery leaves, and chopped onion, and then sauté in a well-heated skillet in a little oil for 2 to 3 minutes.

Sauté the liver in vegetable oil in a frying pan over medium heat for 5 minutes, or when the liver is cooked through. Add the green onions and continue sautéing for another minute. Add the remaining ingredients. Stir well until the liver and green onions are well coated, and serve immediately.

Serves 4 as a side dish.

7 ounces (200 g) beef liver, rinsed well and cut into 1-inch strips
1–2 tablespoons vegetable oil
4 green onions OR 2 Japanese naga-negi (long onion), cut into 1-inch lengths
2 tablespoons white sesame seeds, roasted and ground
1-1/2 tablespoons sugar
2 tablespoons sake
1 teaspoon soy sauce
1-1/2 tablespoons miso

Photo on following page

Yakitori *(YAKITORI)*

Grilled chicken Japanese-style is marvelous with beer or sake, to take on picnics, or for barbecues. The fat drips away in the grilling, and with the addition of green pepper, onions, or cherry tomatoes, it is both nutritious and colorful. Since it is easy to burn the chicken, the pieces may be first lightly pan-fried before skewering. You may substitute beef or pork for an equally delectable kebab—just be sure to have extra sauce on hand.

Cut the chicken and green onions into large bite-size pieces. Mix the sauce ingredients and marinate the chicken and green onions for 15 or more minutes.

Skewer the chicken pieces, alternating each piece with a slice of green onion. Grill over medium flame (or broil in the oven or toaster), basting with the sauce now and then, for 6 to 8 minutes or until the chicken is cooked. Serve sprinkled lightly with red chili pepper and sansho pepper.

Serves 4 as a side dish.

1 lb (450 g) boneless chicken
8 green onions OR 2 Japanese naga-negi (long onion) if available

Sauce:
3 tablespoons mirin
3 tablespoons soy sauce
3 tablespoons sake
1 tablespoon sugar

12–16 metal skewers
Dried Japanese red chili pepper (togarashi) OR hot chili oil
Sansho pepper (prickly-ash powder) OR freshly ground pepper

Photo on preceding page

Chicken Mizutaki *(TORI NO MIZUTAKI)*

One-pot cooking is wonderfully simple yet thoroughly delicious. On a cold winter evening, gathering around the table to cook together creates an intimate, warm atmosphere. *Mizutaki*, like sukiyaki and shabu-shabu, involves cooking a variety of foods at the table in an earthenware casserole set on a portable gas or electric burner (a deep-dish electric hot plate can be a good substitute, if you don't have either one). The food is eaten dipped in a sauce served in individual bowls. You may, of course, put together your own combination of fish, meat, tofu, and vegetables (including precooked carrots, turnips, or mushrooms). Steamed rice often accompanies the meal, although restaurants will serve rice or noodles cooked in the broth. I sometimes have a crusty French bread with this dish—reminiscent of bouillabaisse.

Fill a deep pot with water. Place konbu kelp and chicken pieces in the pot and bring to a boil. Lower heat. Skim surface to remove scum and continue to simmer, until the meat becomes tender enough to fall off the bone. Remove the kelp and transfer chicken and broth to an earthenware casserole or suitable container and bring to the table. Set on a portable heating unit and heat broth to a simmer. Add some of the vegetables and tofu and continue to simmer for 2 to 3 minutes, or until ingredients are tender.

Prepare dipping sauces and serve in individual bowls. Diners serve themselves, dipping the morsels in one of the tangy sauces. Add vegetables and tofu to the pot as necessary.

Serves 4 as a main dish.

5-inch piece of konbu kelp
1 whole chicken, cut into small chunks
1 bunch (300 g) chrysanthemum leaves
    (shungiku) OR spinach
4 green onions OR 2 Japanese naga-negi (long
    onion) if available, cut into 1-1/2-inch
    lengths
1 cake (10 oz/300 g) firm tofu, cut into 12
    pieces

Dipping sauce #1:
3 tablespoons fresh lemon juice
4 tablespoons soy sauce
8–10 tablespoons broth from the pot
2 tablespoons sesame seeds

Dipping sauce #2:
2 tablespoons ginger juice (squeeze from
    freshly grated ginger)
4 tablespoons soy sauce
8–10 tablespoons broth from the pot
2 tablespoons sesame seeds

Photo on following page

Crystal Tofu *(SUISHO DOFU)*

The simplest way of enjoying cold tofu in Japan, called *hyayakko*, is to cut fresh, chilled tofu into large bite-size pieces and eat it with a dipping sauce containing various condiments. It is especially delightful on hot, humid summer days, when appetites yearn for something cool and refreshing. In this dish, the tofu is first dusted with potato starch, boiled, then chilled before serving on a bed of ice. This quick and easy style of preparation gives the tofu a pretty crystal-like appearance and also adds more taste.

Heat dipping sauce ingredients in a saucepan; chill.

Drain tofu (see page 25) and cut into 10 to 12 pieces. Dust each piece with potato starch. In a saucepan filled with lightly salted boiling water, add the tofu pieces and cook 1 minute. Chill in cold water, drain, and place in an attractive bowl over ice cubes.

Prepare condiments. Serve crystal tofu with individual dipping bowls containing sauce and condiments on the side.

Serves 4 as a side dish.

Dipping sauce:
2 tablespoons soy sauce
2 tablespoons sugar
2 tablespoons sake
5 tablespoons dashi broth

1 cake (10 oz/300 g) firm tofu
Potato starch (OR corn starch) for dusting tofu
1/3 teaspoon salt
A bowl of ice cubes

Condiments:
5 green onions, minced
2 tablespoons grated fresh ginger
1 sheet nori seaweed, cut into thin strips

Photo on preceding page

Tofu and Vegetable Scramble *(IRI DOFU)*

This dish is high in protein, inexpensive, and delicious, and can be made with any vegetables you have on hand. Drain the tofu well before sautéing, otherwise you will end up with a watery paste. You may substitute freeze-dried tofu (*koya-dofu*; see package for reconstitution directions). If you add 2 or 3 eggs in this recipe, you will have a tasty variation of scrambled eggs.

In a skillet, sauté the tofu, carrot, and mushrooms in oil over medium heat. Stir in the dashi broth, soy sauce, sugar, sake, and salt. When ingredients are blended, add the string beans. Continue to cook until the liquid has mostly evaporated, then stir in the green onions and beaten egg. Cook until you have the consistency of moist scrambled eggs, and remove from heat. Serve at room temperature.

Serves 4 as a side dish.

1 cake (10 oz/300 g) firm tofu, drained (see page 25)
1 small carrot, cut into julienne strips
2 dried shiitake mushrooms, soaked in water for 30 minutes and cut into julienne strips
1 tablespoon vegetable oil
1/2 cup dashi broth
1 tablespoon soy sauce
2 tablespoons sugar
1-1/2 tablespoons sake
1/4 teaspoon salt
6 string beans, cut into thin strips
2 green onions, finely chopped
1 egg, lightly beaten

Photo on following page

Deep-Fried Tofu *(AGEDASHI TOFU)*

This is an easy-to-prepare, delectable side dish, and a popular feature in lunches or dinners. In place of potato starch to coat the tofu, you may use flour, tempura batter (flour, egg, and water), potato flakes, or almond powder. You can fry the tofu in very little oil, or even do the "frying" in the toaster. Deep-fried tofu goes very well with steak condiments, such as mayonnaise, mustard, Worcestershire sauce, or ketchup.

Dust tofu pieces with potato starch and deep-fry in oil at 340° F (170° C) until a light, golden color. Combine the sauce ingredients in a saucepan, bring to a boil, then remove from heat. Serve deep-fried tofu pieces hot, topped with sauce and garnished with grated daikon.

Serves 4 as a side dish.

1 cake (10 oz/300 g) firm tofu, drained and cut into 4
3 tablespoons potato starch
Vegetable oil for deep-frying

Sauce:
2/3 cup dashi broth
3 tablespoons mirin
3 tablespoons soy sauce

5 tablespooons grated fresh daikon for garnish

Photo on preceding page

Tofu Croquette *(TOFU NO KOROKKE)*

Tofu used in Western-style recipes is no longer unusual, and this dish has become a standard repertoire in Japanese homes. Although ground pork is used here (pork adds just the right amount of juiciness to the dry tofu), you may substitute with ground beef, boneless, lean chicken, canned salmon, tuna, or mackerel.

In a hot skillet, sauté the ground pork, green onions, and carrots in oil. Transfer to a bowl and add the drained tofu, egg, breadcrumbs, soy sauce, salt, and pepper. Divide this mixture into 8 portions and form into patties. Coat the patties with the flour, beaten egg, and breadcrumbs, in this order. Deep-fry in a fryer or suitable skillet 3/4 full of oil at 340° F (170° C) until croquettes turn a crisp, golden brown on both sides. Drain on a rack or paper towels. Blend together the sauce ingredients and drizzle over croquettes. Serve with decoratively-cut radishes on the side.

Serves 4 as a main dish when accompanied by rice, soup, and other side dishes.

2 ounces (50 g) lean ground pork
2 green onions, minced
2 ounces (50 g) carrots, grated
1 tablespoon vegetable oil for frying
1 cake (10 oz/300 g) firm tofu, drained (see page 25)
1 egg
4 tablespoons breadcrumbs
1 teaspoon soy sauce
1/2 teaspoon salt
Pepper to taste

Coating:
6 tablespoons flour
1 egg, beaten
1 cup breadcrumbs

Vegetable oil for deep-frying

Sauce:
3 tablespoons ketchup
2 tablespoons Worcestershire sauce
2 tablespoons water

2 small red radishes, washed with sprouts

Photo on following page

Rolled Omelette *(TAMAGO-YAKI)*

Very popular at breakfast or in Japanese boxed lunches called *obento*, this omelette has a delicate sweet flavor and a pretty layered look when sliced. You may have tried it already at sushi shops, where a thin slab of rolled omelette is served atop vinegared rice, wrapped in a strip of nori seaweed. This recipe can be adapted so that it contains either more or less sugar, and dashi broth may also be added, depending on your preferences. For a colorful variation, try adding chopped parsley to the beaten eggs before frying. Made without sugar, it is delicious in sandwiches and rolled sushi.

Beat the eggs well and blend in the sugar, soy sauce, and sake. Heat oil in a large skillet. Over low heat, add 1/6 of the egg mixture and let it spread evenly over the bottom of the skillet. As the egg becomes half-done, roll it from one edge of the skillet to the other and let it rest on one side of the skillet. Pour a similar amount of the egg mixture into the skillet, making sure it spreads *underneath* the resting omelette roll. When this new layer of egg becomes half-done, fold the first omelette roll inside, rolling from edge to edge. Repeat with another 1/6 of the egg mixture until you have a fairly thick omelette roll. Make another roll in the same way. Slice into thick sections and serve.

6 eggs
2 tablespoons sugar
2 teaspoons soy sauce
2 tablespoons sake
2 teaspoons vegetable oil

Serves 4 as a side dish.

Photo on preceding page

Savory Egg Custard *(CHAWAN-MUSHI)*

Similar in appearance to the dessert, this savory dish is a favorite among young and old alike in Japan. Steamed to a delicate, velvety consistency, it may contain any combination of the following ingredients: shrimp, chicken, fish, mushrooms, ginkgo nuts, tofu, and green vegetables. If you don't have a steamer, select a large pot to hold 4 individual custard bowls or one large custard container.

In 4 heatproof teacups or Pyrex glass containers, place the chicken, shrimps, shiitake mushrooms, and ginkgo nuts. Combine the dashi broth, mirin, salt, soy sauce, and beaten eggs. Pour this mixture into the containers and place them in a steamer or large pot. If using a pot, fill it 1/3 full with water and bring to a boil. Add custard bowls and lower heat to prevent boiling water from entering containers. Cover and steam for 1 minute at high, then lower heat and continue steaming for 13 minutes. Alternatively, place the containers covered with foil in an oven pan containing hot water and cook in the oven at 360° F (180° C). The custard is done when a toothpick or bamboo skewer inserted into it draws out clear liquid. Garnish with cilantro (or mitsuba) sprigs.

*Put ginkgo nuts in a saucepan filled with just enough water to cover them. Cook over low heat for about 5 minutes, then rub the skins off with a spoon.

Serves 4 as a side dish.

3 ounces (80 g) boneless, lean chicken, diced small and sprinkled with sake
4 shrimps, peeled and deveined, sprinkled with sake and soy sauce
4 shiitake mushrooms, trimmed and sprinkled with soy sauce
4 ginkgo nuts, shelled and peeled* (OR pine nuts)
2 cups dashi broth, lukewarm
1 tablespoon mirin
2/3 teaspoon salt
1 teaspoon soy sauce
3 large eggs, beaten
Several sprigs of cilantro OR mitsuba (trefoil) for garnish

Photo on following page

Grilled Eggplant with Ginger and Bonito Flakes

(YAKI-NASU)

Eggplants are at their best from the end of May until autumn, making them an ideal summer vegetable. Since they are bland tasting, it is best to dress them with oil, dried bonito flakes, ginger, and other condiments, or combine them with fish or meat to enhance their flavor and nutritional value.

Grill the whole eggplants on a wire mesh over the stove top (or in a heated, greased frying pan), turning them over regularly. When the skin begins to separate from the body, complete the peeling under running water and pat dry. Make several deep, lengthwise slits from the stem end to the tip of the eggplants. Serve sprinkled with dried bonito flakes, soy sauce, and a small mound of grated ginger.

8 medium eggplants
1/2 cup dried bonito flakes (katsuo-bushi; optional)
2 tablespoons soy sauce
2-inch fresh ginger, peeled and grated

Serves 4 as a side dish.

Photo on preceding page

Simmered Japanese Squash *(KABOCHA NO NIMONO)*

The Japanese squash (*kabocha*) looks like a small pumpkin, with a very hard green skin and bright yellow, sweet meat. For cooking, the skin is usually peeled at random, leaving a decorative effect on the surface and enabling flavors to seep in. If this variety of squash is unavailable, substitute with acorn or butternut squash. You might add poultry or meat to the simmering squash when it is half done (after 5 minutes), to make a delicious main course.

Wash the squash and cut into half. Remove the seeds and the stringy pulp, then cut into 1-inch cubes.

In a pot or Pyrex dish, combine the dashi broth (or water), sugar, and salt. Add the squash and bring to a boil. Cover and lower heat to let it simmer for about 13 minutes, until the squash is tender when pricked with a skewer or fork. Add the soy sauce and serve at room temperature.

Serves 4 as a side dish.

*10 ounces (300 g) Japanese squash (*kabocha*)*
1-1/4 cups dashi broth OR water
3 tablespoons sugar
A pinch of salt
1 tablespoon soy sauce

Photo on following page

Sautéed Burdock *(KINPIRA GOBO)*

This dish of fiber-rich burdock roots has been loved by the Japanese since olden times, and it is frequently prepared at wedding celebrations in some regions of Japan. Julienne strips of these roots are sautéed in oil with carrots and other vegetables, then seasoned with a combination of soy sauce, sugar, and sake. Burdock roots have a strong harsh taste, so soak them first in cold water after scrubbing and cutting them. For a variation, try adding lotus root and sweet potato, or carrots and celery.

In a heated skillet, sauté the burdock root and carrot in sesame oil for 3 to 4 minutes, until tender. Add the sake, sugar, and soy sauce, and continue to cook over medium heat until most of the liquid has been absorbed. Serve with a sprinkling of sesame seeds and chili pepper.

Serves 4 as a side dish.

1 medium burdock root (gobo), scrubbed (or skin lightly scraped), cut into julienne strips, and soaked in water for 10 minutes
1 small carrot, cut into julienne strips
1-1/2 tablespoons sesame oil
2 tablespoons sake
2 tablespoons sugar
2 tablespoons soy sauce
1-1/2 tablespoons white sesame seeds, roasted for 1 minute in a hot skillet
Dried Japanese red chili pepper (togarashi)

Photo on preceding page

Braised Daikon *(FUROFUKI DAIKON)*

Daikon is widely used in Japanese cooking throughout the year, although it comes in season from early winter to spring. Possessing a high water content and a delicate flavor when cooked, it serves as a condiment to many dishes, having helpful digestive properties when eaten with fried or oily foods. In this dish, daikon is boiled in a generous amount of water and served hot with a topping of miso paste. It's especially enjoyable on cold blustery days.

Draw out the bitter taste in the daikon by boiling it in the water used for washing rice. If you are not preparing rice along with this dish, simply slice the daikon and boil until tender.

If you will be preparing rice to eat with the daikon, soak the rice for an hour or two in water. Drain, reserving the water, and prepare steamed rice in the usual way. Bring reserved water to a boil in a saucepan with the daikon. When tender, drain the water and replace with clean water and add the konbu kelp. Bring to a boil, then lower heat and simmer for 8 to 10 minutes.

Combine the ground sesame seeds, miso, sugar, mirin, and water and make into a paste. Serve hot daikon rounds topped with the paste.

Serves 4 as a side dish.

1/3 daikon, peeled and cut into 1-1/2-inch thick rounds
3-inch piece of konbu kelp
3 tablespoons black sesame seeds, roasted for 1 minute in a dry pan and ground
4 tablespoons miso
3 tablespoons sugar
2 tablespoons mirin
4 tablespoons water

Photo on following page

Braised Five Vegetables *(GOMOKU-NI)*

Called *iridori* in some regions of Japan, this dish consists of a hodgepodge of chicken and vegetables, offering an array of colors, textures, and a depth of flavor that appeals to any appetite. Eminently adaptable, it can be part of a feast-laden table celebrating the New Year holidays or used in an *obento* (boxed meal). If you prefer, you may substitute the chicken with beef.

Braise the chicken in soy sauce and sugar in a skillet for 2 minutes and set aside. Heat oil in a large pot and sauté the konnyaku, lotus root, burdock root, and shiitake mushrooms for 1-1/2 minutes. Add the simmering sauce ingredients and bring to a boil. Add the chicken and cook over low heat for about 10 minutes. Next, add carrot rounds and continue to simmer for 5 minutes. When all ingredients are well coated with the simmering sauce, stir in the mirin. This adds a shiny glaze to the dish. Garnish with snow peas and serve.

Serves 4 as a side dish.

6 ounces (175 g) boneless chicken, cut into
    1-1/2-inch pieces

Braising sauce:
1 tablespoon soy sauce
1 tablespoon sugar

1 tablespoon oil
1 block konnyaku, boiled for 3 minutes and cut
    into 1-1/2 inch pieces
1 medium lotus root, cut into 1-1/2-inch
    lengths and soaked in water for 5 minutes
1 medium burdock root (gobo), scrubbed,
    sliced diagonally, soaked in water, then
    boiled for 5 minutes
4 dried shiitake mushrooms, soaked for 30
    minutes and sliced into halves

Simmering sauce:
2 cups dashi broth
3 tablespoons sugar
1-1/2 tablespoons soy sauce
2 tablespoons sake

1 medium carrot, sliced in thin rounds
2 tablespoons mirin
8 snow peas, boiled

Photo on preceding page

Vegetable Tempura *(SHOJIN-AGE)*

Perhaps the first dish that visitors to Japan taste when they come to the country is tempura. When neither meat nor fish is included among the deep-fried ingredients, the dish is called *shojin-age* (derived from the Buddhist term for vegetarian cooking, *shojin ryori*). Although a formal tempura dinner will normally include fish, shrimp, or chicken, this simpler dish is often served by the shrewd Japanese housewife to lure her family into eating vegetables. Leftovers can be served with chilled or hot soba to make delicious tempura soba for another meal.

In a saucepan, bring the dipping sauce ingredients to a boil, then set aside to cool. Pour oil into a Chinese wok or a suitable pot until 1/2 full and heat to 340° F (170° C).

Lightly mix the eggs, flour, and *ice-cold* water in a bowl until ingredients are just blended but the batter is still lumpy.* (If you are using commercial tempura mix, follow package directions.) Test oil temperature by dropping a bit of batter into oil. The batter should sink a little into the oil, then immediately rise up. Mix carrot and string bean strips. Dip these clusters and other vegetables into the batter and fry in the oil until golden and crispy. It is best not to fry too many bunches at once or the temperature of the oil will be lowered. Serve very hot with individual dipping sauce and condiments of grated daikon and ginger.

* Here's a hint for real crispy tempura: while you fry, keep the bowl containing the batter cold by putting it in a large bowl filled with ice cubes.

Serves 4 as an appetizer or side dish.

Dipping sauce:
1 cup dashi broth
3 tablespoons soy sauce
2 tablespoons sugar
1 tablespoon mirin

Vegetable oil for deep-frying

Tempura batter (OR use packaged tempura mix):
1 cup all-purpose flour, sifted
2 eggs
3/4 cup ice-cold water

1 medium carrot, cut into 2-inch julienne strips
8 string beans, halved lengthwise
1 medium sweet potato, sliced into thin rounds
1 medium lotus root, peeled and sliced into thin rounds
1 medium onion, cut into thin rounds
3 tablespoons grated fresh daikon
3 tablespoons grated fresh ginger

Photo on following page

Sautéed Mixed Vegetables *(YASAI ITAME)*

A quick and tasty dish can be prepared using any combination of vegetables and meat (roast beef, ham, bacon, etc.) on hand with this recipe. These sautéed vegetables are delicious over Chinese noodles or udon noodles, or with an omelette.

Season the pork with soy sauce and sake for 3 minutes. Heat oil in a large skillet and stir-fry the ginger and pork over high heat for 2 to 3 minutes. Then add the vegetables that take longest to cook first. When all vegetables are tender, add the soy sauce, salt, and pepper and cook for 1 minute more. Adjust seasoning to taste and serve hot.

Serves 4 as a side dish.

3-1/2 ounces (100 g) roast pork, sliced thin

Pork seasoning:
1 teaspoon soy sauce
1 tablespoon sake

2 tablespoons vegetable oil
1-inch fresh ginger, peeled and in slivers
1 small carrot, sliced thin and boiled
1 medium onion, sliced thin
1/2 medium cabbage, sliced thin
1 large OR 2 small green peppers, in slivers
10 ounces (300 g) bean sprouts
1 tablespoon soy sauce
1 teaspoon salt
A pinch of pepper

Photo on preceding page

76

Braised Hijiki *(HIJIKI NO NIMONO)*

Dark, firm-textured, non-caloric hijiki seaweed is blessed with an abundance of minerals, including calcium and iron. This recipe introduces one of the most popular methods of cooking hijiki, sautéing in oil before simmering in a sweet, soy sauce–based broth. A little hijiki will go a long way, since the dried form will expand 2 to 3 times after being reconstituted in water. Although hijiki cooked in this way is a natural accompaniment to a bowl of rice, I found, quite by accident, that it is delicious in sandwiches or mixed with pasta. Hijiki keeps indefinitely in its dry form, but once it is reconstituted and cooked, it will keep for only 3 days in the refrigerator (longer if the dish is reheated).

Rinse hijiki and soak in water for about ten minutes. Heat oil in a skillet and add well-drained hijiki, sautéing for three minutes over medium heat. Add the sliced deep-fried tofu pouch and the remaining ingredients and simmer for 10 minutes until most of the liquid disappears. Serve warm or at room temperature.

Serves 4 as a side dish.

1 ounce (30 g) dried hijiki
1 tablespoon vegetable oil
1 deep-fried tofu pouch (abura-age), *rinsed in boiling water to remove excess oil and sliced into thin strips*
3 tablespoons soy sauce
3 tablespoons sugar
2 tablespoons mirin
1 cup water

Photo on following page

Sushi in a Pouch *(INARI-ZUSHI)*

This is a simple home-style sushi of vinegared rice stuffed into deep-fried tofu pouches that have been seasoned with sugar and soy sauce. Serve with Spinach Ohitashi, Rolled Omelette, Vegetable Tempura or Breaded Fried Swordfish, and Vegetable Chowder for a complete Japanese meal. For barbecues, Sushi in a Pouch goes well with salads and grilled meats and fish.

Cook the rice (see "Cooking Notes").

Combine seasoning ingredients for sushi rice in a saucepan and briefly heat until the sugar and salt have dissolved. Scoop rice out and mix seasonings into warm, cooked rice, all the time fanning the rice with your free hand. Sprinkle sesame seeds over rice.

Cut the 12 rectangular tofu pouches in two widthwise so you can open them like bags. Immerse them in boiling water, drain and squeeze out excess water, then simmer in a saucepan with soy sauce, sugar, mirin, and water over medium-low heat for 10 minutes or until all the liquid disappears.

When the rice has cooled, shape into balls and stuff each into a tofu pouch and fold over the open end. Eat with pickled ginger on the side.

Serves 4 as an accompaniment to other dishes.

2-1/2 cups short-grain rice (to make 7 cups steamed rice)

Seasoning for sushi rice:
5 tablespoons rice vinegar
2 tablespoons sugar
1 teaspoon salt

2 tablespoons white sesame seeds
12 deep-fried tofu pouches (abura-age)
4 tablespoons soy sauce
4 tablespoons sugar
2 tablespoons mirin
1 cup water
Pickled ginger, sliced thin (optional)

Photo on preceding page

Sushi Mélange (CHIRASHI-ZUSHI)

This sushi recipe incorporates many ingredients into a colorful and nutritious main dish without being full of calories. It is easy to prepare and can be served in one large bowl or platter—great for gatherings. Try adding spinach, green pepper, beans, or fish flakes (such as boned, grilled, and flaked salmon) for a variation.

Cook the rice (see "Cooking Notes").

Combine the seasoning for sushi rice by heating the vinegar briefly so that the sugar and salt dissolve. Pour this over the hot rice and mix in gently but thoroughly, fanning the rice with a fan (or newspaper) with your free hand. Fanning helps to lessen the sourness of the vinegar, adds a glisten to the rice, and prevents it from becoming sticky.

Place the shiitake mushrooms, lotus root, tofu pouch, carrot, and burdock root into a saucepan containing sugar, soy sauce, sake, and water. Cook over medium heat for 10 to 12 minutes or until most of the liquid has evaporated.

Beat the two eggs, mix in the sugar, and make an unfolded omelette sheet. Cut into julienne strips.

Mix in simmered vegetables with the vinegared rice. Serve in a large shallow bowl garnished with thin strips of cooked egg, string beans, and slivers of pickled ginger. Serve at room temperature.

Serves 4 as a main dish.

2-1/2 cups short-grain rice (to make 7 cups steamed rice)

Seasoning for sushi rice:
5 tablespoons rice vinegar
2 tablespoons sugar
1 teaspoon salt

3 dried shiitake mushrooms, soaked for 30 minutes and cut into thin strips
1 medium lotus root, peeled and chopped
1 deep-fried tofu pouch (abura-age), rinsed in boiling water to remove excess oil and cut into strips
1 small carrot, cut into thin strips
1 small burdock root (gobo), scrubbed and soaked in water for 5 minutes, and cut into thin strips

Seasoning for vegetables:
3 tablespoons sugar
3 tablespoons soy sauce
2 tablespoons sake
1-1/2 cups water

2 eggs
1 tablespoon sugar
20 string beans, boiled and cut into thin strips for garnish
Pickled ginger, cut into slivers for garnish (optional)

Photo on following page

Roll-Your-Own Sushi *(TEMAKI-ZUSHI)*

This is a mouth-watering, impressive sushi dish, ideal for small parties. It is easy to prepare and fun to eat. Serve wet towels for wiping hands between making rolls.

Cook the rice (see "Cooking Notes").

Combine the seasoning for the sushi rice. Mix hot, cooked rice with the seasoning, fanning the rice with a fan (or newspaper) with your free hand. Let cool and transfer to an attractive bowl.

Cook the sliced mushrooms in a saucepan with the sugar, soy sauce, and mirin until all the liquid has evaporated.

On a large serving platter, arrange the assorted fillings. Bring this to the table, along with the bowl of rice, the stack of nori seaweed sheets,* extra soy sauce, and wasabi paste. Give each person chopsticks or a spoon and a small saucer of soy sauce with a dab of wasabi paste on the side. To make a sushi roll, take a sheet of nori seaweed and spread a small amount of rice in the center. Dab a bit of wasabi paste onto the rice if sashimi is used in the filling. Lay 2 or 3 filling ingredients on top of the bed of rice before wrapping the contents into a roll. Dip *lightly* into the soy sauce and enjoy.

To help the beginner, here are some suggested combinations:
Sashimi and cucumber
Sea bream and avocado
Ham and rolled omelette strips

*Nori seaweed tends to absorb moisture quickly, so if they go limp, crisp them by waving them over medium heat on the stove top a few times or microwaving in the oven for 40 seconds.

Serves 4 as a complete meal.

2-1/2 cups short-grain rice (to make 7 cups steamed rice)

Seasoning for sushi rice:
5 tablespoons rice vinegar
2 tablespoons sugar
1/2 teaspoon salt

Assorted fillings:
6 dried shiitake mushrooms, soaked in water for 30 minutes and cut into julienne strips

Seasoning for the mushrooms:
1 tablespoon sugar
1 tablespoon soy sauce
1 tablespoon mirin

4 ounces (100 g) tuna sashimi, sliced 1/4 by 2 in.
4 ounces (100 g) sea bream sashimi, sliced 1/4 by 2 in.
4 ounces (100 g) sole sashimi, sliced 1/4 by 2 in.
4 ounces (100 g) squid sashimi, sliced 1/4 by 2 in.
4 ounces (100 g) yellowtail sashimi, sliced 1/4 by 2 in.
4 ounces (100 g) salmon sashimi, sliced 1/4 by 2 in.
4 ounces (100 g) salmon roe (OR smoked salmon)
4 eggs, made into a rolled omelette with 1-1/2 tablespoons sugar and a pinch of salt (see Rolled Omelette, page 60), then cut into thick strips
1 avocado, sliced thick
4 ounces (100 g) ham
1 cucumber, cut into strips
10 sheets nori seaweed, toasted and quartered
Soy Sauce
Wasabi (Japanese horseradish) paste

Photo on preceding page

Rice Balls *(ONIGIRI)*

Rice balls are wonderful for picnics or barbecues because they are compact and can be eaten without plates or utensils, and are good accompaniments to other foods, from salads to grilled meats. Freshly steamed rice is molded into round or triangular shapes, with a filling of salted salmon flakes, dried bonito flakes, pickled plum, or other full, rich-tasting condiment. This recipe introduces two different kinds of rice balls, one made with sesame seeds and the other wrapped in nori seaweed. Leftover cold rice balls without the seaweed wrapping can be basted with soy sauce and toasted to make delicious grilled rice balls (*yaki-onigiri*).

Cook the rice (see "Cooking Notes").

Take half the cooked rice and mix in a bowl with a pinch of salt and the sesame seeds. To form triangular rice balls, place a scoop of rice in one hand and cup with your other hand to pack the rice. Gently rotate the ball in your hand, shaping the sides and edges as you go to form a triangle. If the rice is too hot to handle, use a well-wrung kitchen cloth or plastic wrap and place the rice in the center before shaping.

With the remaining cooked rice, sprinkle with another pinch of salt. To form round rice balls with a filling, scoop a small amount of rice with one hand and with the other hand, place a small portion of salmon flakes in the middle before packing and shaping rice as if you were making a snowball. Wrap a strip of nori around the ball.

Makes 8 to 12 rice balls.

2-1/2 cups short-grain rice (to make 7 cups steamed rice)
2 pinches of salt
2 tablespoons sesame seeds
1 salted salmon fillet, grilled and flaked (OR strips of smoked salmon)
1 sheet nori seaweed, cut into thick strips

Photo on following page

Rice with Bamboo Shoots *(TAKENOKO GOHAN)*

May is traditionally the best time of the year for fresh young bamboo shoots, and this dish is at its best in Japan at this time. Freshly harvested bamboo shoots are soft and may be used as is for cooking. Assuming that you don't live next to a bamboo patch, the bamboo shoot that you buy at the supermarket will need to be boiled before using in cooking. Follow the boiling directions provided. Of course, you can eliminate this process if you use the canned or prepackaged variety.

Preparation:
Remove two or three of the outermost layers of the shoot and cut off an inch from the tip. Make a deep cut lengthwise along one side of the bamboo shoot to its center. (This will enable easy removal of the outer layers after boiling.) Immerse the shoots in water saved from washing rice and bring to a boil. Reduce heat and let simmer for 40 to 50 minutes, or until tender. When cool, remove the skin and allow the shoot to soak in clear water. (Unpeeled, boiled shoots can keep in the refrigerator for three to four days in water changed daily.)

In a saucepan, simmer the bamboo shoots and tofu pouch pieces in dashi broth, soy sauce, sugar, and 2 tablespooons of sake until the liquid evaporates. Place the rice in a pot with the water and 2 tablespoons of sake and bring to a boil.* Lay the cooked bamboo shoots and tofu pouch pieces on top of the rice without mixing and continue cooking. When the rice is done, mix and sprinkle with buds of sansho pepper.

*If you are using an automatic rice cooker, add the cooked bamboo shoots and tofu pouch pieces to the rice from the beginning.

Serves 4 as an accompaniment to other dishes.

7 ounces (200 g) bamboo shoot, chopped small
1 deep-fried tofu pouch (abura-age), rinsed in boiling water and cut into thin strips
1 cup dashi broth
2 tablespoons soy sauce
2 tablespoons sugar
2 plus 2 tablespoons sake
2-1/2 cups short-grain rice, rinsed (reserve rinse water if boiling bamboo shoot)
2-2/3 cups water
Buds of sansho pepper (kinome) for garnish, OR watercress, shiso leaves, basil, or parsley

Photo on preceding page

Salmon and Tea Rice *(OCHAZUKE)*

Here is a dish dating to the old days when cooked, hardened rice was softened with boiling water or tea for another meal. Topped with meat or flakes of fish, this soupy risotto may be eaten at the end of a full-course meal, after an evening of drinking to soothe the stomach, or as a late night snack. Although freshly cooked rice may be used in this recipe, cold, day-old rice is fine, warmed in the microwave or steamed hot.

Grill the fillets, about 4 minutes on each side, until flesh turns opaque and light pink. Be careful not to burn them. Remove the skin and bones, and flake the meat with a fork. Divide the rice into 4 deep bowls. Top each bowl of rice with a portion of salmon flakes. Pour 1 cup of hot tea or hot water over each serving. Top with cut nori seaweed and a dab of wasabi paste.

Serves 4 as a side dish or light meal.

2 salted salmon fillets (about 8 oz/220 g)
3 cups steamed rice (OR cook 1-1/3 cups rice)
4 cups hot Japanese green tea OR boiling water
1 sheet nori seaweed, cut into thin strips for garnish
2–3 teaspoons wasabi (Japanese horseradish) paste

Photo on following page

Chicken Rice Soup *(TORIZOSUI)*

This light gruel can be easily made with leftover rice and vegetables. It is eaten in Japan either for breakfast, a late night supper, or as the finale to a full-course meal. For a satisfying supper, serve with a salad (such as Vegetables with Tofu Dressing), Braised Meat and Potatoes, and Tofu and Vegetable Scramble.

Over medium heat, bring the dashi broth to a boil in a saucepan; add the chicken, shiitake mushrooms, salt, sake, soy sauce, and rice and cook for 3 minutes. When the rice has softened, stir in the beaten eggs. Cook for 1 minute more. Serve hot garnished with mitsuba leaves.

Serves 4 as a light meal or as an accompaniment to other dishes.

5 cups dashi broth
3 ounces (90 g) boneless chicken breast,
    chopped into small pieces
2 shiitake mushrooms, cut into julienne strips
1 teaspoon salt
2 tablespoons sake
1 teaspoon soy sauce
2 cups cooked, cold rice, rinsed with water in a
    sieve and drained
2 eggs, beaten
Several sprigs mitsuba (trefoil) OR watercress,
    chopped for garnish

Photo on preceding page

Beef Donburi *(GYUNIKU DONBURI)*

The donburi, or rice bowl, is a simple and tasty way of stretching ingredients to make a meal for four. One much loved donburi dish in Japan, called *gyudon* for short, is introduced here. Thin, tender slices of beef are simmered with vegetables in a light, mildly sweet broth, then sometimes enveloped in egg, and the whole heaped over a bed of steaming-hot rice, approximating the flavors of sukiyaki (in fact, you may use sukiyaki leftovers). Use freshly cooked rice to allow the broth to be absorbed.

Cook the rice (see "Cooking Notes").

Heat the broth ingredients in a large saucepan. Add the onion and cook over medium heat for 2 minutes until tender. Add the beef and cook for 2 to 3 minutes. Gently break the eggs over the mixture, being careful not to disturb the yolks.

In the meantime, divide steamed rice among 4 deep bowls. When the egg whites in the saucepan have become opaque, scoop out the eggs, with the portions of beef and onions underneath and place each egg and beef portion over the four rice servings. (The eggs may be omitted altogether.) Dribble remaining broth in saucepan over each serving. Garnish with mitsuba leaves.

Serves 4 as a main dish.

2-1/2 cups short-grain rice (to make 7 cups steamed rice)

Broth:
2 cups dashi broth
2 tablespoons soy sauce
2 tablespoons sugar
2 tablespoons mirin

1 medium onion, sliced thin
10 ounces (300 g) sukiyaki beef slices cut into 1-inch lengths
4 eggs (optional)
A few sprigs of mitsuba (trefoil)

Photo on following page

Chicken-and-Egg Donburi *(OYAKO DONBURI)*

Kids in Japan love this particular rice bowl dish. The delicious flavors of chicken and egg in a sweet soy sauce broth cloak a bed of plain, steaming-hot rice, making a satisfying lunch or light supper.

Cook the rice (see "Cooking Notes").

Heat the broth ingredients in a saucepan until the sugar dissolves. Into a small frying pan over low heat, pour about 1/4 cup of the heated broth. Add one-quarter of the chicken and green onions. Cook the chicken pieces, turning them over for about 3 minutes, then beat an egg and stir in. Add a sprig or two of mitsuba and cover the saucepan. In the meantime, have ready one portion of steamed rice in a deep bowl. When the egg has set, in about 50 seconds, slip the mixture over one serving of rice. Sprinkle with nori seaweed. Repeat this process for the remaining servings.

Serves 4 as a main dish.

2-1/2 cups short-grain rice (to make 7 cups steamed rice)

Broth:
1 cup dashi broth
5 tablespoons soy sauce
2-1/2 tablespoons sugar
2-1/2 tablespoons mirin

6 ounces (160 g) boneless chicken, cut into bite-size pieces
4 green onions, sliced diagonally
4 eggs
A few sprigs of mitsuba (trefoil)
Nori seaweed (toasted), chopped for garnish

Photo on preceding page

Pork Cutlet Donburi *(KATSU-DON)*

Another favorite donburi in Japan is crisp, golden-brown pork cutlets married with a strong, flavorful broth. It is very easy to make if you have cold leftover cutlets from the previous night's dinner. If you wish, thin slices of beef may be substituted for the pork, and three eggs may suffice to serve four.

Cook the rice (see "Cooking Notes").

Heat vegetable oil 1-inch deep in a frying pan or wok to 340° F (170° C), or until a few breadcrumbs dropped into the middle of the oil surface immediately. Trim off excess fat from the fillets, pat dry, and sprinkle both sides with salt and pepper. Dust the fillets first with flour, then dip in the beaten egg, and coat evenly with breadcrumbs. Fry in the oil, about 4 to 5 minutes each side, or until golden-brown. Drain on paper towels, then cut each cutlet into 1-inch wide slices.

Mix the broth ingredients in a bowl. Heat one-quarter of this broth in a separate skillet and bring to a boil. Add a portion of the onion and cook over medium heat for 2 minutes, or until tender. Add the slices of one cutlet and cook 1 minute more. When the broth has thoroughly coated the cutlet, pour one portion of beaten eggs into the skillet and stir gently. Add 2 tablespoons green peas and cook for 30 seconds more. Put one portion of steamed rice in a deep bowl, then scoop out the cutlet and egg mixture and place over the rice. Repeat this process for the remaining portions.

Serves 4 as a main dish.

2-1/2 cups short-grain rice (to make 7 cups steamed rice)
Vegetable oil for deep-frying
4 boneless pork chops OR loin fillets
Salt and pepper

Coating:
3 tablespoons flour
1 egg, beaten
1 cup breadcrumbs

Broth:
1 cup dashi broth or water
6 tablespoons soy sauce
6 tablespoons sugar
4 tablespoons mirin

1 medium onion, sliced thin
3–4 eggs, beaten
8 heaping tablespoons green peas

Photo on following page

Three-Colored Donburi (SANSHOKU DONBURI)

This colorful rice dish displays a topping of ground beef or chicken, scrambled eggs, and slivers of snow peas. The meat and scrambled eggs are slightly sweetened, making this a popular *obento* (boxed lunch), well-loved by Japanese children. Vinegared sushi rice in place of plain steamed rice may be used, and sautéed green peas, corn, or carrots also make colorful substitutions for the topping. Try to use freshly cooked rice to allow the juices from the meat to be absorbed.

Cook the rice (see "Cooking Notes").

Sauté ground meat with the seasoning ingredients. Scramble eggs with the sugar. Boil snow peas in lightly salted water and drain. Mound the hot, steamed rice onto four individual serving plates or bowls. On top of each serving, arrange the ground meat, scrambled eggs, and snow peas into three distinct sections. Serve hot or at room temperature.

Serves 4 as a main dish.

2-1/2 cups short-grain rice (to make 7 cups steamed rice)
7 ounces (200 g) ground chicken OR beef

Seasoning for ground meat:
2 tablespoons soy sauce
2 tablespoons sugar
2 tablespoons mirin
1 teaspoon grated ginger

4 eggs, beaten
1-1/2 tablespoons sugar for the eggs
15–20 snow peas, cut into slivers

Photo on preceding page

Chilled Soba Noodles with Nori *(Zaru Soba)*

Soba (buckwheat) noodles with a chilled dipping sauce is the perfect meal for a sweltering summer day (although in Japan, this dish is eaten all year round). This nutritious Oriental pasta dish is light, so there is room to add an accompanying dish or two. You might like some roasted sesame seeds (whole or ground) or thin strips of omelette in the dipping sauce.

Heat the dipping sauce ingredients in a saucepan until the sugar dissolves; remove from heat and chill.

Prepare the chopped onions, grated ginger, nori seaweed sheet, and set out on the table with the wasabi paste. Fill individual saucers with the chilled dipping sauce.

Bring a large pot of water to a boil and add the soba noodles. When the pot comes to a boil again, add a small amount of cold water (about 4 tablespoons) to control the boiling. Reducing the heat prevents the outer covering of the strands of noodles from dissolving. This may be repeated several times until the soba is cooked (the package directions will guide you for proper cooking time). Drain and rinse under running cold water, agitating the noodles gently to remove all starch. Drain well and place on a serving platter. Serve immediately.

Each person mixes in a portion of the table condiments into the dipping sauce. (If wasabi paste is served, dissolve a 1-inch strip from a tube into the dipping sauce.) Everyone helps themselves to the noodles, dipping them first in the dipping sauce before slurping them up.

Serves 4 as a main dish.

Dipping sauce:
1 cup dashi broth
5 tablespoons soy sauce
4 tablespoons sugar
1 tablespoon mirin

Condiments:
4 green onions, chopped
3 teaspoons grated ginger
1 sheet nori seaweed, toasted and cut into thin
   strips
Wasabi (Japanese horseradish) paste (optional)

1 pound (450 g) dried soba (buckwheat)
   noodles

Photo on following page

Summer Udon Noodles *(HIYASHI UDON)*

Udon noodles are made from wheat flour, water, and salt. During much of the year in Japan, they are eaten in a hot broth. In this recipe, the noodles are served in a small amount of chilled, light broth containing soy sauce and sugar (similar to Chilled Soba Noodles) and topped with sliced roast pork and shredded vegetables.

Briefly boil the broth ingredients, then remove from heat. Chill in the refrigerator until ready to serve.

Prepare the omelette strip, cucumber, carrot, and meat toppings and set aside.

Bring a large pot of water to a boil and cook the udon noodles as you would spaghetti, until tender but al dente. (Follow the directions on the package for proper boiling time.) Drain and immediately rinse in running cold water. Drain well and divide among four individual serving dishes.

Top each serving of noodles with a portion of omelette strips, carrot slices, roast pork (or chicken), and cucumbers. Finally, pour chilled broth over each serving. Eat with a dab of mustard mixed into the noodles and broth.

Serves 4 as a main dish.

Broth:
1-2/3 cups dashi broth
6 tablespoons soy sauce
4 tablespoons sugar
4 tablespoons mirin

3 eggs, made into an omelette and cut into thin strips
2 cucumbers, sliced thin
1 small carrot, cut in slivers and boiled until tender
4 ounces (100 g) roast pork OR chicken, sliced thin
14 ounces (400 g) dried udon noodles
Mustard

Photo on preceding page

Japanese Stir-Fried Noodles *(YAKI-SOBA)*

This dish of Chinese-style wheat noodles stir-fried with vegetables is fun food, always sold at stalls around Japanese temples and shrines on festival days. It is simple to make (great as snack fare) and potentially addictive with its uncomplicated, barbecue-like sauce.

Heat half the oil in a frying pan and sauté the pork and vegetables over medium heat for 2 to 3 minutes until tender. Season with salt and pepper. Remove from frying pan and set aside. Heat the remaining vegetable oil and fry the noodles for 3 minutes over medium heat. Return the pork and vegetables to the frying pan and season with Worcestershire sauce and soy sauce. Fry 1-1/2 to 2 minutes more and serve on individual plates, sprinkled with crushed nori seaweed.

Serves 4 as a light main dish or snack.

1-1/2 tablespoons vegetable oil
7 ounces (200 g) roast pork, cut thin
6 leaves cabbage, cut in slivers
7 ounces (200 g) bean sprouts
2 small green peppers, cut in slivers
Salt and pepper
1-1/4 pounds fresh (or 1 pound dried) Chinese-style wheat noodles OR ramen, cooked in boiling water until al dente, drained, and patted dry
4 tablespoons Worcestershire sauce
1 tablespoon soy sauce
Nori seaweed, roasted and crushed (mominori), OR sesame, paprika, or dried parsley

Photo on following page

Savory Supper Pancakes *(OKONOMI-YAKI)*

If you have a portable hot plate, try this dish for a fun, cozy meal with family or friends. These Japanese pancakes are made with flour, cabbage, and diced seafood and pork, brushed with a tasty Worcestershire and ketchup sauce, and garnished with shredded nori seaweed. Japanese regional specialties include one version stacked one on top of the other, and another with Chinese-style noodles sandwiched between the pancakes. Experiment by adding or substituting small bite-size pieces of squid, octopus, or grated yam to the pancake batter. Sprinkling bonito flakes on the cooked pancakes adds an extra special flavor.

Mix flour, eggs, pork, cabbage, half the shrimps, and a pinch of salt in a bowl until you have a thick, smooth batter. Heat a small amount of vegetable oil on a hot plate or frying pan and pour the batter on it. Cook over medium-low heat for 5 minutes, or when you see small bubbles form around the edges. Place the remaining shrimp on the pancake and flip over to cook the other side, for about 2 minutes. Brush the cooked side with the Worcestershire and ketchup sauce and sprinkle powdered nori seaweed on top. Try eating the pancakes piping-hot, with a dab of mayonnaise, straight from the hot plate.

Serves 4 as a main dish.

1/4 cup all-purpose flour
4 eggs
8 ounces (227 g) roast pork, cut in slivers
10 large cabbage leaves, cut in slivers
*1 cup dried shrimps (*hoshi-ebi*), OR bite-size*
    pieces of your favorite crustacean
A pinch of salt
1-1/2 tablespoons vegetable oil
4 tablespoons each Worcestershire sauce and
    ketchup
*Nori seaweed, in powdered form (*aonori*), OR*
    *dried bonito flakes (*katsuo-bushi*)*
Mayonnaise (optional)

Photo on preceding page

Mochi Cakes with Sweet Soy Powder *(KINAKO MOCHI)*
Mochi Cakes Wrapped in Nori Seaweed *(NORIMAKI MOCHI)*

Mochi is cooked glutinous rice (sometimes known as sweet or sticky rice), pounded into a mass and shaped into rectangular or round cakes. They are traditionally served in Japanese New Year's soup, and are also sometimes eaten in place of steamed rice at meal times. Don't let the compact size of the mochi fool you into overindulgence, however, since one cake (5 oz/150 g) is equivalent to a bowl of rice in calories! Mochi cake is delicious eaten as a snack or dessert, two recipes for which are given here. Since they become dry and hard quickly, serve them as soon as possible. Plain untoasted mochi cakes keep well in the freezer. Simply defrost for 10 minutes to serve them next time.

For Mochi Cakes with Sweet Soy Powder, combine the soy powder with a pinch of salt. Toast the mochi cakes in a toaster or on a wire mesh over the stove top for 6 to 7 minutes, or until they puff up. Be careful not to burn them. Immerse briefly in boiling hot water until soft. Drain and place the cakes on serving dishes. Coat generously with soy powder and sugar and serve immediately.

To make Mochi Cakes Wrapped in Nori Seaweed, toast the mochi cakes as described above, then sprinkle with soy sauce. Toast the nori seaweed sheet by passing it several times over medium heat on the stove top until it turns crisp and aromatic. Cut into quarters or eighths and wrap a strip around each mochi cake. Serve immediately.

*Soy powder here refers to flour made from roasted soybeans, light gold in color and ready to eat as is.

Serves 4 as a snack.

8–12 cakes mochi
3/4 cup soy powder* (kinako)
A pinch of salt
4 tablespoons white sugar
2 tablespoons soy sauce
1 sheet nori seaweed, cut into quarters

Photo on following page

Dessert Rice Balls *(OHAGI)*

Since olden times, these glutinous rice balls, covered with mashed, sweetened azuki beans or ground, black sesame seeds, were made for religious festivals in spring and fall. Nowadays, these dessert rice balls are eaten throughout the year. The balls are not too sweet—and for the health conscious, the good news is that azuki beans are rich in iron and minerals. You may find it convenient to use commercial, presweetened azuki bean paste, although it tends to be sweeter than homemade paste.

Wash and rinse the glutinous rice and place in 1-1/3 cups of water. Let it soak for two hours, and proceed as you would with white rice. When rice has cooled, shape into small balls with your hands.

To make the azuki bean paste, place beans in a saucepan filled with water and bring to a boil. Drain and add 3 cups fresh water and cook, uncovered, over low heat. After about 1 hour, add 1/2 cup cold water. This will break the skin of the beans and speed up their softening. When beans have softened, add the sugar and a pinch of salt and continue cooking until the liquid has evaporated. (This will take about 10 to 15 minutes. Check often to prevent burning.) Remove from heat and mash with a large spoon.

Take plastic wrap or a clean, well-wrung kitchen towel and place about 2 to 3 tablespoons azuki paste on it. Place a rice ball on top of it and wrap, twisting the paste over the rice until it is covered with the bean paste. Repeat to make 6 to 8 rice balls.

For rice balls with sesame seeds, combine the roasted, ground sesame seeds with sugar. Roll each rice ball in this mixture until it is completely covered.

Keep dessert rice balls under plastic wrap at room temperature until ready to serve. Leftover portions may be kept in the freezer, either in freezer wrap or a tight-lidded plastic container. It's best to avoid storing in the refrigerator since the rice balls will become hard.

1-1/2 cups glutinous rice (mochi-gome)

With azuki bean paste:
1 cup azuki beans
1/2 cup sugar (add extra if you would like to keep finished rice balls for a couple of days at room temperature)
A pinch of salt

With sesame seeds:
3 tablespoons black sesame seeds, roasted for 1 minute in a pan and ground
1 tablespoon sugar

Makes 12 to 16 small rice balls.

Photo on preceding page

White Dumplings *(SHIRATAMA DANGO)*

This is a simple, slightly sweet snack made with only a few ingredients—yet delicious! The miniature dumplings are made from glutinous rice flour, boiled, grilled, and enveloped in an aromatic brown sauce made from a cooked blend of soy sauce, sugar, and mirin. A time-old Japanese recipe, the dumplings are also served coated with chilled fruit and syrup, or covered with azuki bean paste. You might like to Westernize it by using chocolate sauce or your favorite homemade jam for the coating.

Add the water to the rice flour and let it soak for a few minutes. Mix together into a dough and divide into 12 portions. Shape each into a round dumpling. Boil a pot of water and drop the dumplings one by one in it. They will sink at first, but when they rise to the surface, boil for one minute more, then drain and immerse immediately in cold water. (This helps to firm up the dumplings.) Drain well.

Heat the soy sauce, sugar, and mirin in a saucepan over medium heat for 1 minute, or until the sugar dissolves. At this point, if you prefer a thicker sauce, blend in the corn or potato starch and remove from heat.

Skewer the dumplings 3 to a stick, and grill on a wire mesh over medium heat until the surface becomes evenly brown. Brush the brown sauce over the dumplings and serve.

Serves 4 as a snack.

1 cup glutinous rice flour (shiratama-ko*)*
1/2 cup water

Brown sauce:
2 tablespoons soy sauce
2 tablespoons sugar
2 tablespoons mirin
1 tablespoon corn OR *potato starch (optional,
    for a thicker sauce)*

4 bamboo skewers

Photo on following page

Deep-Fried Sugar Cookies *(KARINTO)*

These sweet, crispy cookies are made from a light pastry dough, deep-fried, and coated with white or brown sugar icing.

In a bowl, sift the flour and baking powder. Blend in the sugar, a pinch of salt, egg, and milk. Make a smooth dough and roll out super thin on a cutting board. Cut into 1/2 x 1/4-inch thin strips. (Sprinkle the dough with flour if it is difficult to cut.) Heat vegetable oil in a wok or deep skillet 1/3 full to 330° F (165° C). Drop the pieces of dough into the oil one at a time, taking care that they do not stick together. Take the cookies out when they are evenly browned and drain on a paper towel.

Make the icing by heating the brown sugar and water in a saucepan over medium heat, stirring throughout, until it thickens. Test thickness by taking a small dollop of syrup on a fork and immersing it in a glass of water. If it hardens in water, it is ready. Place the fried cookies into the saucepan of syrup and stir gently until all pieces are coated evenly. Transfer to a lightly greased aluminum tray and allow to cool.

If white sugar icing is desired, simply replace brown sugar with an equal amount of white sugar.

Makes 20 to 30 cookies.

1 cup all-purpose flour (OR ready-made pancake mix)
1 teaspoon baking powder (omit if you are using a ready-made mix)
1-1/3 tablespoons brown OR white sugar
A pinch of salt
1 egg
3 tablespoons milk
Vegetable oil for deep-frying

Icing:
1/2 cup brown sugar
2-1/2 tablespoons water

Photo on preceding page

Sweet Potato Twists *(CHAKIN SHIBORI)*

These charming twisted dumplings made of puréed sweet potato hide a delicious filling of whole sweet chestnut. Marshmallows or nuts also make good fillings.

Bring out the yellow color of the sweet potato by peeling the skin thick. Cut into 1-inch rounds, then soak in water for about 2 hours to eliminate any raw, bitter taste.

After soaking, rinse the sweet potato pieces and boil in water until tender. Drain and mash (or purée) while still hot. Add the sugar, butter, and vanilla essence. Divide into 8 portions. Take a well-wrung, thin muslin kitchen cloth (not a towel), or aluminum or plastic wrap, and place one portion of the mashed sweet potato mixture in the center. Press with your thumb or spoon to flatten it, then place a chestnut in the center of this. Wrap up and twist. Repeat for the remaining portions.

Serves 4 as a dessert.

14 ounces (400 g) sweet potato
3 tablespoons sugar
1-1/2 tablespoons butter
1–2 drops vanilla essence
8 whole chestnuts, preserved in syrup

Photo on following page

Index